Freelance Programming For Profit

Robert Plank
&
Thom Lancaster

Printed in the United States of America

The content for this book is sourced mainly from training seminars carried out by Robert Plank, and is used under license.

Dedicated to Internet Marketers everywhere, with thanks.

Freelance Programming For Profit

Table of Contents

About The Authors

Robert Plank is a 26 year old home-owner from California. He is a full time Internet Marketer and PHP programmer.

To find out more about Robert, visit RobertPlankTraining.com.

Thom Lancaster is a UK based Internet Marketer. He has a particular interest in product creation.

To find out more about Thom, visit ThomLancaster.com.

Foreward

If you're looking to get into freelancing programming, then you could do far worse than by following Robert Plank's example.

Although Robert is now a top level Internet Marketer and information product creator, he's also an excellent programmer, and is particularly well know for his many varied PHP products.

Robert has had a lot of success with his programming for clients, and I'm very pleased that he's sharing his system – the

RobertPlankTraining.com

Freelancing Attack Plan – here with you in this book.

Do take a careful read and apply everything, and in particular look at how you can be paid more when you follow Robert's simple steps.

I wish you well.

Thom Lancaster
ThomLancaster.com

Chapter 1 - Introduction

Hey guys, I've made good money as a freelance programmer, and a lot of you have asked me how you get started as a freelance programmer. That's how I got started, and maybe you already are doing freelancing but you're going about it the wrong way.

If you're doing on freelance sites, you're doing it wrong, at least if you're doing it on freelance sites for a while. The point of getting on freelance sites is to take up a few small jobs just so you can build up a reputation as someone who does good work, just for the proof, for the social aspect of it, for the testimonials.

You take these jobs on freelance sites so you can get happy reviews for starters, so you can send people to this page and say "look at all these reviews." And you can get contacts so that you can get repeat business -- maybe from the people who you already did work for or maybe those people will recommend you to others.

That's it. As far as I'm concerned, that's all the freelance sites are good for. Because, otherwise, if you stay on them, you'll end up spending the rest of your life doing bidding wars. And you'll be bidding against people from India, against people from the Philippines, against people from South America, who have a very different exchange rate as you. And they'll be able to bid down $5 or $10, and to them that's a lot of money. To you, that's definitely not even worth your time.

You don't want to stay there forever, but that's a good place to start -- better than most places. And once you get a reputation, forums will get you the best freelancing jobs over time where you cultivate a relationship.

Chapter 2 – Getting Money Right Away

I was just thinking about this while I was driving today is what would I do if I really had to start over and I needed some immediate money. What I would so is I would find somebody who needed work done in a skill that I was very, very good at that not a lot of people were good at, and that I could do a lot of easily without getting tired. I was just thinking I would try to get jobs doing Camtasia

PowerPoints for people because many people have articles, but they don't know how to make them into videos and how to market those videos.

I would say, "Give me any of your articles." Maybe I'll just start it off at $7, and I would say, "If you give me a hundred of your articles, give me 700 bucks, and I will go through each one and make each article into a three to four minute video."

You can't just come out and say that. You need to find people looking for that, but I've seen many people looking for that. So I know that that's a real need, and that's what I would do if I had to start over.

Hopefully that's kind of where you are, where you're really good at doing something with programming. Like you're really good with WordPress or really good with Drupal or really good at just making these really quick-fix solutions or just something. You have a specialty that not a lot of people have because if you have a specialty that everyone else has, it's not a specialty. And that's where you're going to be competing based on price.

If you're competing based on price, that means that the only unique thing you have to offer is a low price, and you don't want that. You want the only unique thing you have to offer is your unique skill so that you can charge more.

Chapter 3 – Getting Started On Freelance Sites

If you're doing this day-to-day, first you have to get started on that freelance site. You have to get the social proof in. So on the first day bid on a freelance site; so you need to get at least a little bit of experience, at least one contact under your belt if you have no contacts, if you have no reputations on the forums or whatever.

Find one single project by browsing through Elance, RentACoder, ScriptLance -- just pick one of the three main freelancing sites. Because you don't want to say, "Go to this site for these reviews and this site for these reviews." Just pick one site and bid on jobs at it. You can say, "Look, I have ten reviews on RentACoder." Let's say you were on RentACoder. You want to find one single project that would take you two hours or less to do.

So if some guy said, "I need you to do a script that does this and this and this, and that's it." If you looked at it and said it would take two hours, then you would accept that project at any price, because you're not going this first project for money. You're doing it so that you can get used to accepting a project and getting the script done and turning it in.

Don't take on any new projects until that one is finished and submitted. So this should be something that you can get done in one or two sittings. You're just going for that first review, because it's so hard to win a bid with zero reviews. Even one or two reviews is way better than zero.

So the first day you've done just that one project. On the second day, actually look at the price. So bid on a small project again -- four hours or less preferably, so something you can do in an afternoon -- and think about how much is your time worth. Is it worth 20 bucks an hour? Is it worth 50 or 75 an hour? Then look at how long the job would take, and then that's usually how much you should place as your bid.

So the point is to get more reviews and contacts just like yesterday, but this time get paid for it. You're never going to get paid very well at a freelance site. I know some people who get paid very well as freelancers, but that's not on a freelance site. Those are people who started at a freelance site and found a good contact and kept getting work from him, and then just kept jacking his rates up as he had more proof, as he had more experience, and as he just was able to work more efficiently.

But the thing about doing freelancing is you want to take on small stuff. So when you're first starting out you want to have it so that at the end of each day, you are 100 percent done with your work. It's not, "It pretty much works, but I got to do this one thing tomorrow." It should be you're 100 percent done with your work. I know that's not always possible, but you need to try to be hitting that goal.

Chapter 4 – The 'Double Up' Strategy

Now you're onto day 3, it's time to try something new.

Try try to double up projects. So maybe this is on a weekend or something. You want to try to bid and win on two projects both that you can complete in a day. So this will get you used to having two projects in the air at a time. Because later down the road you're going to be just focused on the one project. You finished it. Then you open up another project, but then the guy comes back and says, "Can you make this one extra change?" or "Can you fix this one thing?" And then you're going to have to juggle multiple projects; so it's good to see what that's like.

Get used to the schedule of having two projects in the air at a time. Maybe you'll devote the morning to project 1 and the afternoon to project 2. Maybe one hour to project 1 and one hour to project 2, whatever works for you. But what you want to do is you finish the smaller project at full speed so you can complete the second project by day's end. And I said "complete," not start or work on.

You repeat that for one week. You keep trying out one project a day, two projects a day for a week to get some solid reviews.

For this to work you need to be doing this every day. You can't skip a day. You can't skip every other day. It has to be every day for a week, because otherwise you're going to end up having take in three projects or four projects. But if you do it like this, you'll end up having taken ten projects. And if you hit each one of those guys hard for a good review and a good rating, then you'll get ten good ratings and ten good reviews.

Later down the road when you're trying to get new clients, you can say, "Here are all of my reviews. Here's all the people who said I was the best programmer they ever had, who said I was fast, who said the turnaround time was a couple of hours."

Chapter 5 – The Freelancing Mindset

What you've done so far will get you into the freelancing mindset. There's just some things that you need experience for, so you should prepare for it if you graduate later from freelancing into making your own products or something. Then if you really need money, if you're in an emergency, you should have a place to go and run to and take a couple of freelance jobs to pay the bills.

That will get your brain to tackle all of the usual problems most people have when joining freelance sites when they don't know how much to charge. They don't know how to start and finish a project quickly. They don't know how many projects to bid on. You'll have conquered all of those problems in your one week. You'll have figured out, "Well, I did this job and I did this work, but I felt like I was underpaid." So that means next time you need to bid more. Or maybe you're bidding too high and you realize people aren't accepting my bids. They're always going with someone cheaper; so you need to lower your bid. Remember you're not going to be living on these freelance sites forever, just maybe a couple of weeks. So it's okay if you charge a little bit less than your worth.

This will just give you an idea for if you have to go back to this, you'll already be experienced with that. It just really sucks if you have a limited amount of time to get a certain amount of money. You don't have time to learn new things. You learn it now so that if you need to go back to it later, you already know it.

Chapter 6 – Forum Networking

Now that you've got your reviews and you've got a few contacts, maybe you've already got some repeat work coming from the freelance stuff, you join a forum and start networking. The really good forums for getting programming jobs done or for getting work as a programmer is either -- a programming forum is probably the least helpful out of this three I'm listing because many of them will try to solve problems on their own, but you can still get work from a programming forum. But the best ones are the webmaster forums and the site building forums. So something like WebmasterWorld or SitePoint or Digital

Point -- those are great way to find good jobs as freelancers. But you have to look a little bit more.

With the job sites it's right in front of you, but with the forums maybe people are -- you have to find the right thread and you have to be the first person ever to find it before someone else does. You need to just get in contact with people on a one-to-one basis and try to get work that way.

But however you get your work, even though it's going to be a little more difficult, you'll get paid more and you can link to your freelancer profiles for reviews so the people can see that you do a good job. Then when you're on the forum, you can make it easy for people to contact you. You don't have to wait for somebody to post a job for you to go and take work. People can come to you.

How do you get forum jobs? Many forums have a help needed section where people post programming errors, where they offer jobs to fix scripts or to write a script from scratch or to fix a web site or to make a web site from scratch and so on. And many forums have a special offer area where you can offer a limited number of slots.

Sites like the warrior forum and Digital Point let you write offers where you can say, "I'm a programmer, and I have three slots available. So if you want me to take on your programming project, get in now because I've only got 3 slots. And here's the proof so here's my link to the freelancing site where I have all my reviews. Here's the price I charge by hour, but if you give me your project details, I'll be able to figure out how many hours it'll probably take me, and then I'll give you a quote with how much it'll probably cost you."

Basically you're writing a sales letter and you didn't even realize it. You're adding in elements of benefits and proof and scarcity and all that good stuff. So you're selling yourself. And just like any sales letter, you don't want to be too generic. You don't want to be selling them all the solutions to their problems. You specify a special problem they have and a specific solution. So you're going to want to specialize yourself.

You don't want to try to sell all different kinds of services like "Oh, I can do this language and that language and I can reformat your sites, and I can do HTML and I can submit your sites to the search engines." Just pick one thing you can solve. So do you write full scripts from scratch? Do you write simple scripts? Do you fix existing scripts? Do you take scripts that totally work and install them? There's big money to be made in taking scripts like WordPress or taking forums or something and installing them with certain plug-ins and customizing them to the way people want them to work.

What language are you programming in? Do you program in PHP, JavaScript, ASP .NET, Joomla!, or WordPress? It doesn't necessarily have to be a language. It can be an actual script.

And what price do you charge, and is your price per hour? Is it per day of work or is it per project? Or is it a mixture of the two?

The point is be unique because all the other programmers are going to be vague and they're going to say "Talk to me. We'll figure out a quote. I do all these languages. I do all these services." You can say, "No. I just do this." Then if somebody has a job that perfectly fits you, you can say, "This is perfect because I've done this every single day. These are the only kinds of jobs I do."

Then when you post your special offers you can say, "All I'm offering is WordPress installs" or "All I'm offering is simple PHP scripts that take one day or less to make." So what you're doing over time is you're being specialized and you're building clients. You're going to reuse them from the freelance sites and from the forums.

If they really like you, they will recommend you to others. It's important that they do. Usually it'll just happen on its own. It's important because all clients will eventually go bad. Eventually they just will move to a different programmer or they'll stop doing what they're doing or maybe you'll have a falling out or maybe you'll get sick of them. Whatever.

You're not going to be working for that person for the next 10 or 20 years. You'll be working for them for the next few months maybe or maybe the next year or two, but very rarely any longer than that. And that's just the way things work. You're not taking a full-time job with them. You're just doing things for them on a project to project basis.

Chapter 7 – Building Reputation

When you're marketing on forums and you're trying to build up a reputation and trying to sell yourself, there are a few tactics you can use.

The first tactic you're going to do is set up a simple web site. So once you've been at this several weeks and you've got all the reviews, see if your name -- like my name is Robert Plank -- see if yourname.com is available. If it is, register it and set up a single-page site explaining what you do. You say, "This is what I charge. This is the language I do, and this is what I'm best at -- this particular task -- like installing or fixing whatever or making WordPress themes or installing your WordPress themes or customizing your WordPress themes, whatever."

The only info you should have on your simple web site are your 4 to 8 skills, your portfolio -- so those reviews or those sites you worked on -- the rate you charge, and how to contact you. That's it. Don't list a billion different skills. Don't tell them that you can scan their documents or do transcriptions or do voiceovers. No one's going to read all that stuff, and it's going to distract them. It's going to make them think you're a Jack of all trades and master of none. You want to be the expert in what they're looking for.

If you list your phone number and your address on the page, then you'll show up in the search engines. Many people are looking for local programmers. So I get hits to my site all the time on my resume, and I used to get job offers all the time until I changed my resume to say something like -- you know like in your resume at the top you have the objective line, and my objective was "My job needs are being fulfilled at this time. Please don't contact me ." But before then I was getting job offers every week from companies in the East Bay and the Bay Area near Silicon Valley.

Just the fact that you're listed in Google gives you a leg up over most over freelance programmers, because most other freelance programmers don't have a single site of their own up. All they do is click on the freelance job boards all day. And the next level up for that is the guys who wait around on forums all day looking for work, but nobody sets up a simple web site. If you set up a simple web site, then people are coming to you and then you have the upper hand. You can negotiate a certain price, and they will be more desperate to buy from you because they came to you and they already invested this time into trying to get a job from you. So you get paid more if you have a web site. It's just that simple.

Chapter 8 – Overflow Agreements

Here's how you capitalize on relationships.

The next tactic you can try is an overflow agreement. So by now you must have networked with some of your fellow freelancers, not just people looking for work, but other people giving work just like you in the same situation as you.

What you can do is talk to these guys and you say, "I'm a newbie. How about we arrange a deal so that if you get a job and you're busy, you can refer people to me? That way you're not leaving them hanging. That way you're not taking in too many projects. And if you want, I'll do the same thing to you."

Most of the time people will say yes. Most of the time you don't even need to give a commission for that. It's totally okay just because they don't want to leave people hanging who come to them for solutions because they don't want people to start going to somebody else. And at least if they go to you, this person can keep tabs on you and they're not just going off to some stranger. There should be a little level of trust if they know you and they're laying out their reputation on the line. At least they can try to contact you if you're unreachable. Or if the person you work for has a complaint, at least they can go to that other programmer. So just get another freelancer to give you his overflow requests for work.

RobertPlankTraining.com

Chapter 9 – Getting Paid More

You need to be looking to increase your price. So start out low to get the jobs, and then if you finish your work quickly and keep your clients happy, you can keep bumping up your price.

And if you do it slowly enough -- maybe at first you take on a job for 500 bucks, and then you take on a job for 700 bucks. Then you take the same job later on for a thousand bucks. If people stop doing repeat work for you, that's fine. You've still got massive amounts of proof, and you still should be able to get jobs. Maybe you have to put in 5 percent more effort to get the job, but you have to justify that quote by breaking down why. "I put in this many hours of PHP coding, this many hours of database coding, and this many hours HTML coding. I charge a different rate for each one." Maybe you have to be a little bit more convincing. Maybe you have to throw in a few extra bonuses like, "I'll throw in a bonus on how to use the script once you're trying to install it so that you have less customer support issues.

Or I'll give you three months of very minor changes," and so on. So, the bigger your portfolio, the more you can charge. You're going to want to charge more eventually as you get a portfolio built up. It's really tough to do, but once you do it you'll be glad you did.

Chapter 10 – The Publishing System

This seems kind of counterintuitive, but it works.

You need to release an e-book. So if you're really good at something, teach somebody else how to do it. Most people won't even bother to learn how to do it. So if you're really good at how to secure WordPress and your unique selling proposition is "Not only will I set up

WordPress for you, but I'll install all the plug-ins and I'll do all the small customizations to the script to make it more secure."

Then you write a quick book about how to secure WordPress. Your first thought is, "Well, if people learn how to secure WordPress, then they're not going to want to pay me." And you'd be wrong. Because if somebody is looking for that information anyway -- how to do it themselves -- they'll find it. And if they don't find your book, they'll find someone else's.

And then the second thing is that, again, it goes back to Google. If someone is looking for the guy to set up WordPress and make it secure, your name is going to come up as one of the first results because you have an e-book. If you have an e-book, you look a lot more credible than a person who's just offering this service. You say, "Not only do I offer this service, but I also have proof that I know how to do it because I've written the book on it." Everybody thinks that you're an expert on something just because you've written the book.

Write a simple report in your niche -- you're talking about WordPress security, about how to do some simple drag-and-drop stuff in C#, how to install scripts, how to write Joomla! plug-ins, 7 easy ways to solve this common problem. Whenever I'm stuck about what e-book to write about, I just think about what's a really tough problem that I always see when I'm on the forums looking for freelancing, what's the common problem that always comes up?

And then what's a couple of easy ways to solve that problem. So you just write a report about that, and now not only can you get traffic from the search engines, on those forums where you're posting every day and building up a reputation, if people ask that you say, "Here's my free report or here's my $7 report that tackles that issue."

You want to have a call to action at the end of that book with ways to contact you for freelancing. Everybody I know including myself who's gone from freelancing to report creation, we've given up freelancing forever because it's just really stressful to do for too long of a time. We put out e-books now on the same subject, and we still have people requesting if we do freelancing even with no call to action.

I can't even imagine if you sold a couple hundred copies of an e-book if you had a call to action at the end of how to contact you for freelancing, you'd always be busy. If you go the e-book route, make sure you have a call to action at the end of the book saying, "By the way, if you want to contact me for freelance work, go to this URL or send me an e-mail here and we'll work something out."

Chapter 11 – Advanced Tactics

I’ve got a few more freelancing tips to share with you.

Always get paid 50 percent up front. You don't want to agree to something and you put in all the work, and then the guy disappears or he pays you less than what you want. Maybe you will get paid less than what you wanted but at least you'll get that first half. So it's always good practice. And if somebody doesn't want to pay you 50 percent up front, then you can say, "Look at my reviews. I have good reviews. That's proof that you can trust me." If they still don't want to pay you 50 percent up front, you tell them it's a deal breaker. If they still say no, then you don't do work for them. So don't do work without 50 percent up front.

Get good at writing air-tight specifications so clients can't sneak in features later. Once you get the hang of freelancing, you notice that it doesn't matter how quickly you can make something. They'll want you to make this script, and you'll make it and it'll be almost done. It'll be 90 percent of the way done, and they'll say,

"By the way, can you throw in this feature?" That totally delays this project.

Or maybe you'll get the first version done and it'll be totally out of your brain, and they'll say, "By the way, can you add in this feature?" And then when they do that, then you say, "All right. Pay me this extra amount of money, and we'll do it."

Don't get carried away with crazy ideas and features. Know your limits. But just doing those first few projects on the freelance sites will guarantee that you can look at what somebody says they want a script to do, and then you go back to them and say, "Okay, this script will do exactly this. And when you go on this screen, all they can do is click on this link, this link, or that link. And when they go to this page, all they can do is this, this, and this, and they can't do this." You be very specific about what they cannot do, because you don't want to get stuck in the contract and keep doing more and more work even though you're only paid once. Because if you're paid once and you keep doing more and more work, then the amount you are paid per hour keeps decreasing. You don't want that.

Chapter 12 - Summary

The freelancing attack plan was you start with small jobs on the freelance sites to get reviews and contacts. You move to forums. You accept jobs people might post on forums, and you give your own special offers that people can come to you.

Don't be afraid to charge what you're worth. Yeah, you're going to have to start charging a small amount, especially when you're competing against overseas traffic.

But once you get the reviews and once you find your groove, once you know what you're really good at, you can become specific and charge more.

Don't be afraid to ask your old clients if they need any work done because most of your work is going to be coming from old clients, which is a very good thing, because you already know who's the people that you like to work with and who don't you like to work with. So you can make sure that you always work for people that you like.

And then tactics you can use once you've got the freelancing ball rolling -- you set up a simple web site so that you can list your 4 to 8 main skills and show your proof and have it easy for people to contact you.

You arrange overflow deals with other freelancers; so if they're totally booked up and somebody comes to them, that freelancer will refer the job to you.

You can increase your price over time and release an e-book for lead generation. So you release an e-book on the same subject as stuff you freelance about to get some buyers, so people will buy from you, so people will recommend you, and that will lead to even more freelance work.

RobertPlankTraining.com

Chapter 13 - Conclusion

Thanks for reading this book. That was how to get started as a freelance programmer. I hope that was helpful for you even if you aren't a freelance programmer.

If you're a freelance anything, some of this stuff doesn't apply -- like the stuff with the specifications -- but then again, it kind of does. Say if you're an article writer, you need to make sure to specify that articles are a certain length and articles contain this percentage of keyword density and only have this much research applied to it. So it's kind of similar, but I think the biggest takeaway from this is just don't spend the rest of your life on freelance sites.

Graduate up to repeat clients where you can charge more. Graduate up to being on forums and being cleverer where you can do these things like release e-books and joint venture with other freelancers to get work. So just be smart about it. Work smarter, not harder.

Robert Plank
RobertPlankTraining.com

www.ingramcontent.com/pod-product-compliance
Lightning Source LLC
Chambersburg PA
CBHW021859170526
45157CB00005B/1887

* 9 7 8 1 4 6 1 1 1 3 5 0 8 *